Spotlight on
Prehistoric Mammals

Tim Wood

Franklin Watts
London · New York · Sydney · Toronto

© 1988 Franklin Watts

Franklin Watts
12a Golden Square
London W1

First published in the USA by
Franklin Watts Inc.
387 Park Avenue South
New York, N.Y. 10016

Franklin Watts Australia
14 Mars Road
Lane Cove
NSW 2066

Phototypeset by Keyspools
Limited
Printed in Hong Kong

UK ISBN: 0 86313 687 7
US ISBN: 0–531–10542–3
Library of Congress Catalog
Card Number: 87–51476

Illustrations:
Mike Atkinson
Robert and Rhoda Burns
Elizabeth Graham-Yooll
Michael Welply
Bernard Long

Photographs:
David Bayliss RIDA
Imitor
Survival Anglia

Design:
Janet King
Peter Luff

Technical consultant:
Dr Richard Moody

Note: The majority of
illustrations in this book
originally appeared in
Prehistoric Mammals,
A First Look Book.

Contents

The first mammals

200 million years ago the Earth shook with the tread of giant dinosaurs. They hardly noticed the tiny, shrew-like animals feeding nervously among the bushes at night. These animals were the first mammals. Unlike the dinosaurs, the mammals were warm-blooded and their bodies were covered with fur. When the dinosaurs died out these mammals replaced them.

The Earth 200 million years ago. Shrew-like mammals ate insects and eggs.

4

The rise of mammals

This early mammal had teeth like a rat. It ate tree bark, nuts and seeds.

The dinosaurs suddenly vanished 65 million years ago. No one knows why this happened. Life was better for the mammals when the dinosaurs had gone. They no longer had to hide. There was plenty of food to eat. Many new kinds of mammals appeared. The Age of Mammals had begun.

An early
rhinoceros and
ancestors of
the horse.

A prehistoric
wolf.

7

Plant eaters

Many prehistoric mammals ate plants. Some could chew only soft grass. They died out when tough grasses began to grow instead.

An ancestor of the elephant. It lived 30 million years ago.

This strange creature was the same size as a camel but had a short trunk rather like an elephant.

An ancestor of the armadillo. It was protected by a bony shell.

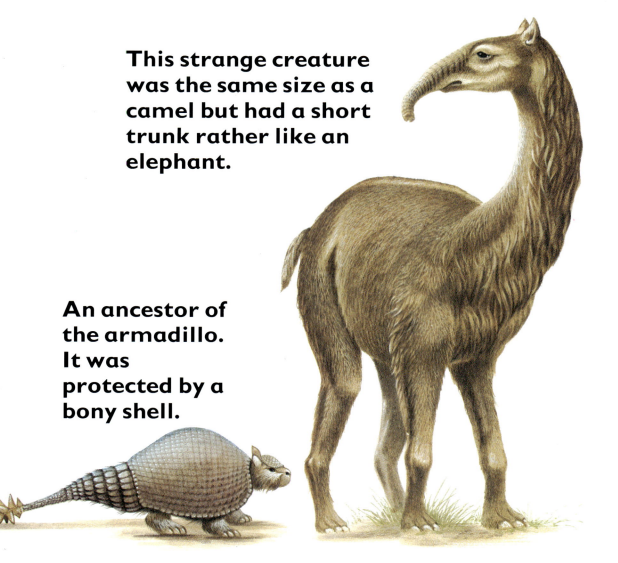

Many plant eaters grew long legs to help them escape from the meat eaters. Some had tough skins to protect them. Others were safe because they grew so big.

Meat eaters

Some meat-eating mammals were quite small and ate only insects. Others grew very large with powerful teeth and sharp claws.

A sabre-toothed cat keeps a pack of wolves from the rhinoceros it has just killed.

Among the fiercest were the sabre-toothed cats. They had two long, sharp teeth shaped like swords. These could easily stab through the thick skin of a rhinoceros.

Giant mammals

A long-necked rhinoceros compared to an elephant.

Some prehistoric mammals grew giant-sized. There were hedgehogs as big as foxes, and pigs as big as cows. There were kangaroos three metres high and sloths the size of elephants. The largest land mammal was a long-necked rhinoceros.

**Giant American sloth
(6 metres long)**

**Giant Australian bear
(just over 3 metres long)**

Swimming and flying mammals

Not all prehistoric mammals lived on the land. Some, like whales, were able to live in the water. Others, like hippopotamuses, spent part of their lives in the water and part on the land. One mammal, the bat, learned to fly.

One of the first whales.

The hippopotamus is related to the pig. It lives in water during the day but feeds on land during the night.

The bat is the only mammal which can fly properly.

Our ancestors

Humans belong to a group of mammals known as primates. The first primates lived in trees. Some stayed there, becoming monkeys or apes.

Ape-like creatures similar to our ancestors.

An early human.

Others, including our ape-like ancestors, began to live on the ground about 14 million years ago. They learned to walk upright.

Evolution

Today's mammals are descended from prehistoric mammals. As the Earth changed, the animals changed too.

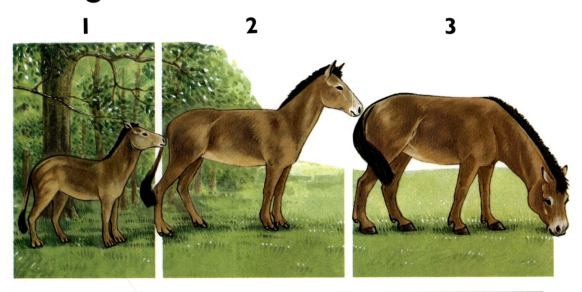

1   2   3

1 **Hyracotherium: lived in swamps 50 million years ago.**

2 **Mesohippus: lived in North America 40 million years ago.**

3 **Merychippus: a grass eater which lived 25 to 5 million years ago.**

The new mammals were better suited to the new conditions. The old mammals died out. This is called evolution. The way the horse has changed over the last 50 million years shows this well.

4   5

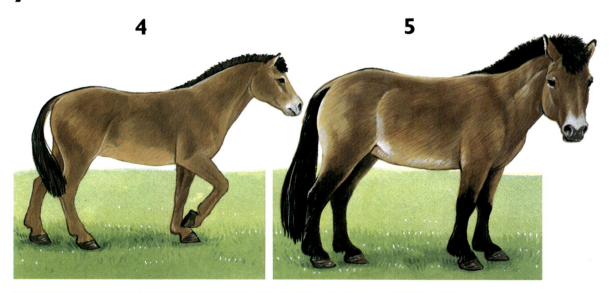

4 Pliohippus: the first hoofed horse lived 5 to 2 million years ago.

5 Equus: the modern horse.

The Ice Ages

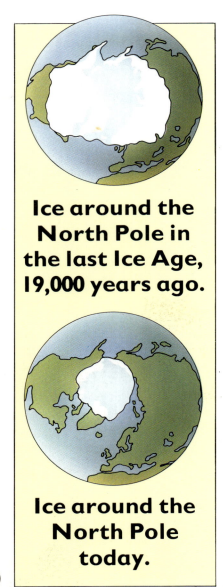

Ice around the North Pole in the last Ice Age, 19,000 years ago.

Ice around the North Pole today.

There have been several Ice Ages during the last 2 million years. Many other animals became extinct, but mammals adapted to survive the cold. As the ice spread from the North Pole, some mammals moved to warmer areas. Others grew thick, woolly coats or lived in caves.

Ice Age mammals.
Woolly mammoths,
woolly rhinoceros,
bears and reindeer.

Unusual mammals

Millions of years ago, Australia broke away from the rest of the world. Some unusual mammals lived there. These were the mammals which carried their young in pouches and mammals which laid eggs. These strange mammals, which died out almost everywhere else, were safe in Australia and still survive there.

The duck-billed platypus. An Australian egg-laying mammal.

A kangaroo mother keeps her baby safe in her pouch.

European mole

These moles look very similar but they carry their babies in different ways.

Australian marsupial mole

The success of mammals

Mammals have spread all over the Earth because they are cleverer than other animals. Mammals can keep their own bodies warm, so even if the weather is very cold, they can still move fast. They can learn new ways to find food and to escape from danger.

The cleverest group of mammals are the primates. The group includes humans, apes and this early lemur.

Many plant-eating mammals have learned to move fast. They often live in herds for extra safety.

Wolves have learned to hunt in packs and share their food.

Fossils

Scientists know about prehistoric mammals through looking at fossils. Fossil teeth can show what sort of food an animal ate. Fossil leg bones can show whether an animal crawled slowly or ran fast.

How fossils are formed.

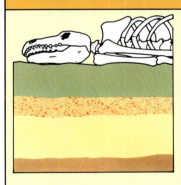

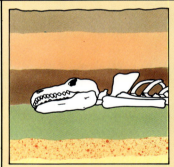

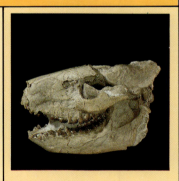

Dead animals' bones are covered very quickly by sand or mud.

After millions of years, the bones are buried deep in the Earth.

They turn to rock. Scientists dig them out and study them.

The fossils of mammoths, wolves and sabre-toothed cats have been found in tar pits in America. The tar has preserved their bodies.

The mammal family

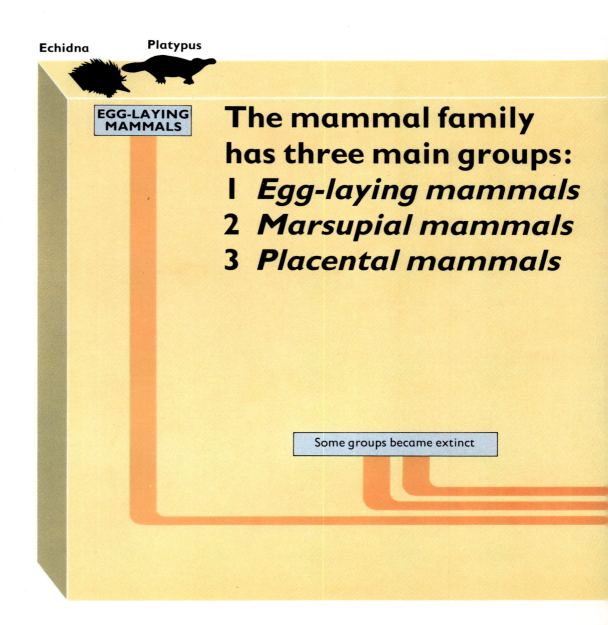

Echidna

Platypus

EGG-LAYING MAMMALS

The mammal family
has three main groups:
1 *Egg-laying mammals*
2 *Marsupial mammals*
3 *Placental mammals*

Some groups became extinct

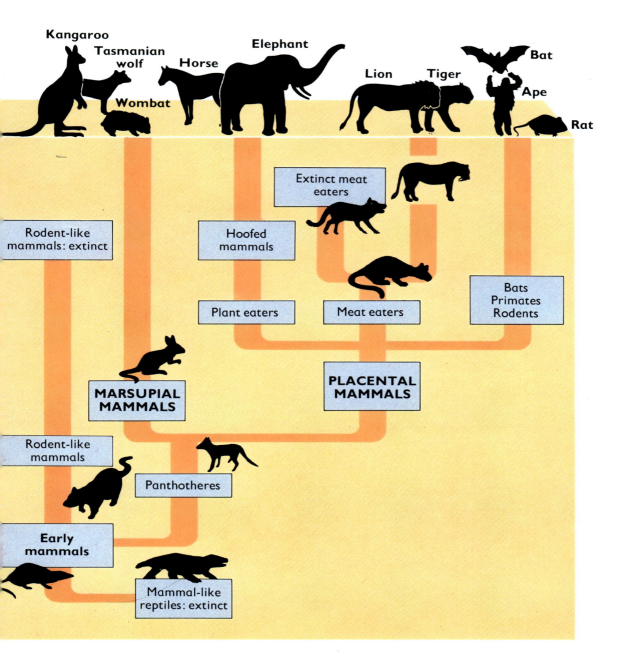

Kangaroo

Tasmanian wolf

Wombat

Horse

Elephant

Lion

Tiger

Bat

Ape

Rat

Extinct meat eaters

Rodent-like mammals: extinct

Hoofed mammals

Plant eaters

Meat eaters

Bats
Primates
Rodents

MARSUPIAL MAMMALS

PLACENTAL MAMMALS

Rodent-like mammals

Panthotheres

Early mammals

Mammal-like reptiles: extinct

29

Prehistoric mammals facts

The largest ever land mammal was a long-necked rhinoceros. Its eyes were nearly 8 metres off the ground.

Megistotherium was the largest meat-eating mammal. Its head was twice as large as a bear's and it often attacked elephants.

The largest deer lived 3,000 years ago. Its antlers were over four metres across.

Some prehistoric mammals were dwarfs. The first horses were the size of cats and the first elephants were the size of sheep.

The largest prehistoric elephants were twice the size of modern elephants.

The smallest prehistoric elephants lived on Malta about 1 million years ago. They were 80 cm high.

The longest tusks ever discovered belonged to a prehistoric elephant in Germany. They were five metres long. This is nearly twice as long as the tusks of living elephants.

Modern elephants eat leaves from trees. Deinotherium, a prehistoric elephant, used its downward growing tusks as a fork to dig for roots.

About 5,000 mammoths have been found preserved in the ice of Siberia in Russia. Sometimes the food in their stomachs is preserved as well. One had been dead for 30,000 years but was fresh enough to be eaten!

The remains of over 4,000 prehistoric mammals were found in one tar pit at La Brea in the United States.

The remains of over 30,000 cave bears have been found in one cave in Austria.

Glossary

Here is the meaning of some of the words used in this book:

Egg-laying mammals

A rare group of mammals who lay eggs. They are found only in Australia.

Evolution

The slow change and improvement which takes place in animals and plants as the conditions on the Earth change.

Extinct

This word is used to describe groups of animals or plants which have died out.

Fossils

The remains of dead animals or plants which have been preserved. Fossils have usually turned to rock, but the remains of complete animals have been found in tar pits, bogs and even deep-frozen in Arctic ice.

Mammals

Animals which feed their babies with their own milk.

Marsupial mammals

Mammals whose mothers carry their young in a pouch in their body. They are mostly found in Australia.

Placental mammals

The largest group of mammals. The young are carried inside the mother until they are born.

Prehistoric

Before written records were kept.

Primates

Group of placental mammals which includes monkeys, apes and people.

Index